TEN Things To Do

In A Conceptual

Emergency

Graham Leicester

Maureen O'Hara

International Futures Forum

'The men of experiment are like the ant, they only collect
and use; the reasoners resemble spiders, who make cobwebs
out of their own substance. But the bee takes a middle
course: it gathers its material from the flowers of the
garden and of the field, but transforms and
digests it by a power of its own.'

Francis Bacon

bee-ing

missing elephant

The Conceptual Emergency

WE live in the age of the missing elephant. The American psychologist Don Michael was first to point out the implications of a world of boundless complexity, rapid change and uncertainty for the familiar tale of the blind men who if they could only pool their knowledge would have recognised the elephant. No longer. In today's world there is little chance that any of us will ever know more than one small piece of the elephant, and there are now so many different pieces, they change so rapidly and they are all so intimately related one to another, that even if we had the technology to put them all together we would still not be able to make sense of the whole.

The world we have created has outstripped our capacity to understand it. The scale of interconnectivity and interdependence has resulted in a step change in the complexity of the operating environment. These new conditions are raising fundamental questions about our competence in key areas of governance, economy, sustainability and consciousness. We are struggling as professionals and in our private lives to meet the demands they are placing on traditional models of organisation, understanding and action. The anchors of identity, morality, cultural coherence and social stability are unravelling and we are losing our bearings. This is a conceptual emergency.

One very human response is to give up the struggle to make sense of what is going on and to lapse into short term defensive strategies or longer term despair. Another is to strive to regain the comfort of control and coherence by reasserting old truths with more conviction and urgency, stressing fundamentals, ignoring inconvenient information, interpreting complexity in simple terms.

These responses can offer temporary adaptation and will quell anxiety for a while. But they can also dissolve into maladaptive neurotic and even psychotic routines. However understandable and human these responses are, they are pseudo-solutions, ultimately doomed to failure.

Not all responses to challenging times are dysfunctional. It is possible to face up to challenge and grow with and through it. Changed circumstances can be seized as opportunities for creative engagement and rather than generating resistance, generate a step change in learning and growth.

IFF, the International Futures Forum, is an international and multidisciplinary group originally convened in 2001 to come up with some touchstones of theory and practice to support a transformative response to today's powerful times and to restore effectiveness in action. The following pages describe ten of the strategies that have emerged from this work to date: ten things to do in a conceptual emergency.

Design for transition to a new world

The world we now inhabit is like nothing we have known before. So different are the challenges of today from the world our schooling prepared us for we are all strangers in a strange land.

A troubling gap has opened up between the demands placed on us and the mental capacities most of us have to deal with them. Research in the workplace suggests that 60% of positions now require a range of intelligences that fewer than 30% of the population possess. Even the best educated are in over their heads. We are entering a new and uncharted land – some of us as intentional immigrants, most of us as refugees.

The only natives in this new world are the young. For them in particular we have a responsibility, having gained an inkling of the direction we are heading, to redesign our schooling and other cultural processes to cultivate the psychological capacities, knowledge and modes of action that will be at home in this new world.

How? By recognising that the needs of the economy, the needs of society and the needs of the individual are converging. In all three spheres the challenge is the same: to grow whole people, people able to take effective action and make meaning from their lives.

We will also need to address the casualties of this cultural shift - and there will be many. California Senator John Vasconcellos says we must become hospice workers for the dying culture and midwives for the new. We have done this before at the dawn of the industrial age when thinking in philosophy, science and the arts was translated into curriculum, social policy and community organisation. Will we show the courage to do so again - this time on a global scale?

TRY OTHER WORLDVIEWS ON FOR SIZE

THE universal circumstance of life is now interconnected, fast-changing and uncertain. There is nowhere to hide from this new context. In every nation is the mystery of all nations.

Throughout history cultures have developed ways of thinking and behaving that fit the worlds they inhabit. In the West we grow people with minds well adapted to the demands of life in an industrial context. We have favoured a worldview based on intellectual mastery, hierarchical and linear logics and quantification.

Other cultures have drawn on different mental traditions, some stretching back thousands of years, in which rationality plays a less central role and where relational networks and circular logics take priority in organising thought, identity and society. Some like Japan and Korea have been hugely successful in adapting to the industrial paradigm while others, among them tribal and indigenous societies, have been less successful in partaking of the fruits of industrial culture and are falling further and further behind.

People in all societies now find that living well in the new global context requires deep changes in consciousness - new minds for new times. The new stance connects synthetic skills such as imagination and intuition with analytic skills of quantification and rationality. It embraces the relationship between embodied knowledge and codified knowledge and reclaims capacities such as storymaking, faith, emotion, empathy and love as essential elements of knowledge. Such expanded capacities also provide ways to feel less overwhelmed, more fulfilled and more psychologically whole so as to thrive as persons and communities in powerful times.

Maintaining a sense of identity and integrity in the new multicultural context, feeling at home in a world of many beliefs, many truths, many realities, will require that we approach diversity in a new way - not a clash but a dance of civilisations.

pilot fish

the f●g at the bottom of the mountain

Re-perceive the present

Pierre Wack was the first leader of Shell's scenario planning team in the early 1970s. But his work was not about predicting the future. He described his role as like leading a pack of wolves, scouting ahead and helping the pack get a better understanding of the landscape around them. He called this the gentle art of re-perceiving the present.

When things change there is a natural tendency to read the new environment in terms that are reassuringly familiar. In orienteering this is called 'bending the map'. Those who admit early that they are lost have a greater chance of survival.

We cannot hope to make perfect sense of the buzzing confusion around us, but we can do a much better job of finding our bearings. We can take a longer term perspective – recognising that our sense of the future and of the past inevitably colour our reading of the present. And we can start to see and take notice of more of the context around us.

Most of us are unaware how much we limit what we notice through preconception, inattention, mindset and cultural habits. Our reliance on numbers and objectivity has downplayed other ways of knowing that are more subjective: knowledge gained from experience, from intuition that we cannot justify, from emotional response, from esoteric levels of consciousness, from the aesthetic arts, poetry and music, from the science of qualities rather than the science of quantities.

It is no accident that the root of 'ignorance' lies in 'ignoring' what we cannot or will not see. Knowledge lives in the darkness and the mystery as well as the light. And it lives, vitally, in relationship and context. In order to know better where we are, we should strive to see as far, as wide and as deep as possible.

Trust subjective experience

MODERN science is grounded in the conviction that in order to know the world reliably we must remain removed from our subjective human experience, which is too vulnerable to bias and self-deception. We should trust instead objective, reproducible, impersonal data generated through methods that distance the observer from the observed. The expert investigator is subject and the world – including the human world – is treated as object.

More recently quantum physics, psychology, philosophy, ecology and social sciences are all starting to highlight the impossibility of the view from nowhere and the unavoidable personal dimension in all knowing. Contemporary science increasingly accepts that knowledge is a human creation and we must account for the effects of our participation in our inquiry. The theory of Gaia for example, the earth as a living system, recontextualises humanity as part of a wider ecology rather than its master and cartographer: we are in nature, not outside it.

The implications for how we see the world and our place in it are profound. When we regard our condition as a participant in a communion of subjects we can no longer reasonably see other people as objects to be organised, managed, abstracted, governed, observed. As the great systems theorist Sir Geoffrey Vickers observed, 'human systems are different'.

Once human subjectivity is reclaimed as an essential and legitimate dimension of all knowledge we can give the same kind of value to the qualities of subjective experience that we have up to now reserved for the abstractions of objective science. From multiple directions we see evidence that deep down the worldview of our society is shifting – from a subject-object view of the world to a subject-subject one.

Take the long view

Systems scientists tell us that structure drives behaviour. We live in 'business as usual' structures that have grown up over decades, accumulating power, resources, attention and prestige. They have become dominant precisely because of their success. It is in the nature of powerful systems to argue for their own survival – and we are forced to act accordingly.

Taking a longer view, we know that business as usual fades and new ways of operating, more fitting with the changed environment, eventually take over. The challenge is to introduce these new ways in the presence of the old. Simple innovation is not enough: it can too easily be captured and coopted by the failing dominant system to prolong its life. We need instead transformative innovation – innovation that paves the way to a different future.

In nature we find that time is an infinite resource, only physical resources are limited. But we operate on the opposite assumptions. Nature's way of coping with uncertainty is to diversify, and every move is provisional. We tend to standardise, looking for short term economies of scale, and yearn for certainty when we should put our faith in learning.

In unknown territory we need a compass not a map, something to give us overall direction and purpose. We will find that compass not in the surface layers of change but deep in the culture where values live.

Expanding our view to include a longer timescale means we must also confront our individual mortality, imagining a world beyond our presence in it. We relish beginnings, innovation and growth. We shy away from endings, closure and withdrawal and do not manage them well: the closing of a factory, the end of an industry, the last days of a life in medical care. Might we find new responsibility in acknowledging the natural life cycle of birth, growth, death and regeneration?

TAKE INSIGHTFUL ACTION

In an otherwise interconnected world, one of the most recalcitrant distinctions we draw is between thinking and action. We see thinkers and doers in different camps. But in a world of rapid change this is a false distinction and a disabling one. We need to redesign the plane whilst flying it.

The capacity to make sensible judgements leading to wise action in conditions of complexity, uncertainty and rapid change does not depend on data and information, or even a set of scenarios. It depends on shifting the model we have in our heads of how the world works closer to reality. We call this insight.

It is the nature of powerful insight that it is hard won, but appears obvious once seen. It reconfigures the world, such that action on the old view becomes intolerable. The more inclusive the view of the operating environment it derives from, the more powerful it is likely to prove in focussing effective action. The ideal is to provide the depth of perception and clarity enjoyed by the martial artist, enabling an exquisite economy of effort about where and when to strike with maximum effect.

Insight is not an abstract idea: it is a way of perceiving the world and it lives in individuals. It cannot be 'transferred' in the way we pretend we can transfer knowledge. But it can be shared. Participative processes generate insight; and subsequent iterations of the process can allow others to experience the moment of insight, sometimes with even greater force.

Insight is not a one off. Insight demands action, which in turn will bring something new into the world and provide the source for new scanning and fresh insight. This is a learning cycle. We cannot plan but will learn our way into the future.

redesigning the plane

Form and support new organisational integrities

We are pushing at the limits of traditional organisation. The rise of partnering, alliancing, outsourcing, cross-cutting and 'joined-up' working creates organisations in which the density of internal transactions is less than the density of transactions with the external environment. The boundaries of organisation are dissolving - a shift critically enabled by technology.

Structures are no longer primary. In a natural ecology it is the flow of energy through the system that creates structure, which in turn configures the flow. Like a whirlpool in a stream, or the standing wave in a skipping rope. And flow in nature tends to evolve more and more complex structures.

Taking effective action in this landscape is more complicated than aligning a group of employees around the corporate mission and the five year plan. That model cannot cope with today's multicultural moment, a world in which all individuals sit in a web of overlapping connections and loyalties, and in which talent needs organisations less than organisations need talent. We have looked to the network to fill this gap, but are left wondering what holds a network together and gives it coherence and identity?

The new organisational structure is a pattern of relationships that is able to maintain its integrity over time. It has the discipline to perform the ordinary as well as the extraordinary tasks, can support a sense of moral purpose beyond its own survival, is open and inclusive, nurtures and supports its members in a challenging environment, and pays generous and caring attention to the demands of the old culture while midwifing the new. The discovery of this form (and it will be discovered not invented) will be a critical advance for all sectors – and our work suggests we are likely to find it first in the arts.

Practise social acupuncture

We assume that big problems need big solutions. But we know that in today's operating environment big actions simply lead to bigger unintended consequences. The 'Manhattan Project' approach to large social challenges is not only bound to fail, it also spreads the disheartening message that nothing on a smaller scale will do.

That is not true. You cannot control complex systems, only disturb them. And even a small disturbance, artfully designed, can have large systemic effects. We call this 'social acupuncture'. Think of Muhammad Yunus walking into a small village in Bangladesh thirty years ago with a few dollars in his pocket. His offer of microloans, against the advice of banks, governments and economists, was a small, disruptive act. It has generated global systemic impact.

We have a far better understanding today of how these effects are obtained if we see society as a complex organism, a living ecology, a social network, or a 'holarchy'. Each 'holon' in a living system is viable in its own right but it also grows in ways consistent with the patterns of coherence of a larger whole. Understanding the world holonically offers a very different approach to planning large scale projects, enabling them to grow more naturally and providing viability at all stages.

For the most part we remain trapped in a world in which top down doesn't work and bottom up doesn't add up. In India they talk about the relationship between the buffaloes and the fireflies – the big bureaucracies and corporations and the small scale social entrepreneurs. We know that fireflies swarm and synchronise. But how much more effective and sustainable might that activity be if the heft of the buffaloes could play a collaborative part? A critical task of modern governance is enabling buffaloes and fireflies to learn better together.

TODAY'S relentless pressures leave many of us feeling overworked, overwhelmed and often cynical. We are bombarded with political and media messages about crisis, terror and impending planetary collapse. Small wonder that in many communities across the globe there is a lack of faith in the future.

This suggests an urgent cultural imperative. Sustainability looks like a limited goal, mere survival. If we really wish to mobilise the energy for change we must ask and answer 'survival for what'? Our answer need not be final, a single vision of the good life or a specific planetary utopia, but somehow we must rekindle hope for a better life in the future.

The philosopher Jonathan Lear tells the story of Plenty Coups, chief of the Crow Indians at the end of the 19th century as his tribe came under pressure to give up their way of life. It was a moment of cultural crisis: 'when the buffalo went away the hearts of my people fell to the ground, and they could not lift them up again'.

But inspired by a dream, Plenty Coups kept his people attuned to changing conditions and guided them through the transition to find a new way of living. Lear calls this 'radical hope' – the hope for cultural rebirth, but without any predetermined vision of what that rebirth will look like.

IFF has not invented the age of confusion – it is a lived reality that resonates with real people around the world, overwhelmed by seemingly intractable problems, impenetrable complexity and bafflingly rapid change. This is the spirit of the times, the theme of history. We need ways of engaging with this theme that are radically hopeful, and new language and stories to counter the drum beat of pessimism. In place of the networks of terror we must build networks of hope.

be fun to be around

Emergency Response: the 'ten things to do' in practice

THE previous pages outline ten strategies for responding to today's conceptual emergency. These strategies are derived from IFF's learning from experience over several years working with others to take on complex challenges.

IFF's role has been one of imaginative catalysis, generating fresh insight. This is not an inert role. Insight emerges only if all the participants are fully engaged and open to learning. We have been changed by our own experiments. That is inevitable. But in the process we have learned what it takes to provide the enabling conditions for strategic insight to emerge and to engage in effective action in these powerful times.

In essence IFF offers a process of iterative learning in conceptual emergencies:

- bridging disciplinary silos
- integrating short, medium and long term perspectives
- alternating systemic broadening out and reflective focusing.

It is a carefully designed and facilitated conversational and 'languaging' process (frame, reframe, insight, projection) based on:

- open-ended joint exploration, including among deeply informed people
- tolerance for and engagement with multiple worldviews / values
- mobilising both codified knowledge and lived experience (embodied knowledge)
- use of narrative knowledge bridging theory and experience
- use of appropriate thinking and learning models and tools as and when required or helpful.

The process continues until new insights emerge and a coherent shared platform for joint action is created.

In developing this work we have sought to operate in circumstances where the emergency is evident - where paradox, ambiguity and complexity characterise the landscape, where new frames and new language are needed to outgrow old mindsets, where rapid change means yesterday's solution no longer works, where long term needs require a long term logic, and where only genuine innovation has any chance of success. We have explored these conditions initially in Scotland, where IFF has its home, and increasingly elsewhere in the global context.

Here are seven illustrative stories from the world of practice, and a footnote on the enabling conditions for success.

BP Grangemouth and My Future's in Falkirk

IFF thrives on paradox – where both X and Y are needed and they seem mutually incompatible. In early 2002 BP Grangemouth refinery in central Scotland faced such a paradox. They had decided to cut up to 1000 jobs from the plant to increase productivity and restore global competitiveness, yet they knew this would depress the local economy on which they also depend. In response, BP joined a partnership with Falkirk Council and the local enterprise agency in which each would make a financial contribution and develop a strategy to transform the local economy. This became the 'Falkirk Action Plan' – an ambitious set of proposals designed to leverage an initial £23m to attract an additional £200m investment over 10 years. But how could such ambition be delivered?

What IFF came to see over the course of an intensive engagement in the region was that at the heart of this Action Plan, although it contained the boldest possible initiatives, was another paradox. For plans are inherently limiting. It seemed based on an underlying model in which the experts had come up with the answers and the only challenge was for the people of Falkirk to put them into practice. If it failed it would be the people's fault, not the Plan's. But that is not how to operate in the complex world, seeking to shape the world and the people in it to your will: quite the opposite.

What IFF did at every turn was to look at the language, the attitudes, the processes, the structures, the mindsets that were limiting or risked limiting Falkirk's aspirations – and ways to make sure that they did not do so in the future.

What has happened since has been astonishing. The Plan was redesigned and launched as 'My Future's in Falkirk' (MFiF) – no longer a plan but a rallying call, an invitation, a spirit. IFF has remained involved as the spirit has spread. Four years into the programme investment had already reached close to £1bn, five times the stretch goal dreamed of in 2002. MFiF has picked up numerous awards, notably for socially responsible business practice. In 2004 it was one of six global finalists for BP's prestigious Helios award, and the only one nominated in two separate categories: partnership and innovation.

BP and Falkirk invited IFF's international network to return to Falkirk in 2007, five years after our original immersion. We were told that we would find a place that 'looks better, feels better and thinks differently'. And we were asked to address a new set of questions. Has Falkirk really transformed? If so, how has this success been achieved? And what should Falkirk pay attention to now as it navigates its way into the future?

This follow up encounter prompted the partners working in Falkirk at all levels to recalibrate their ambition. Economic transformation, it turned out, had been the easy bit. They are now ready to use the spirit they have developed and their collective capacity to think differently to embrace social and cultural aspirations for transformation as well. IFF helped to articulate the spirit of MFiF in participants' own words as a set of prompt cards, making it easier to carry that spirit into other areas: 'Make it personal'; 'Free some resource for the imagination of others'; 'Every project is a cultural intervention' etc.

MFiF is operating at the visionary edge of practice within a traditional political and bureaucratic culture. Its success to date is a case study of the ten things in action; and IFF's engagement continues to provide powerful pragmatic learning for conceptual emergency response everywhere.

Fireflies, buffaloes and India's future

AT the invitation of one of our members, Arun Maira, IFF held its seventh week-long plenary session in India. It was a great opportunity to investigate the challenges of leadership, governance and social change in a huge and diverse nation finding its place in a globalising economy.

Arun Maira and his friend and colleague Rajiv Kumar, chief economist of the Confederation of Indian Industry, flew into our session direct from Davos where they had presented a set of scenarios for the future of India. The scenario of more inclusive, bottom up, sustainable growth based on the entrepreneurship of the fireflies was called 'Pahale India' - India First. The World Economic Forum's detailed economic modelling showed that, surprisingly, this actually promised higher economic growth than any of the other scenarios. But if the fireflies are going to grow India, then what should the buffaloes do? And how can a diverse, huge democracy develop on this model as fast as it needs to when there is no precedent to copy?

IFF set about immersing itself in these questions in a series of learning journeys to diverse settings in and around Delhi. In three groups, we each visited a government agency, a civil society/ community project and, to understand the view from other ways of knowing, an artist.

Each visit was full of insight. The artist who told us of how he wished he had been able to utilise the virtues of Indian classical aesthetics – balance, rhythm, beauty, vitality etc – in his previous work as an economist at the World Bank. The heartening discovery that fireflies exist in government bureaucracies too. The evident joy we saw on people's faces even in the midst of squalor.

Everywhere we went we saw the diligent practice of fireflies building networks of hope, administering social acupuncture. One remarkable organisation we visited was Parivartan, a community movement against corruption set up by Arvind Kejriwal, a senior income tax official on leave from his position. The organisation mobilises communities to use the Right to Information (RTI) legislation to fight corruption and secure the benefits that are rightfully theirs. The RTI legislation is a powerful enabler, an acupuncture point into the bureaucracy.

Parivartan demonstrated that money is often not the most important ingredient for change. It shuns official funding and prefers small individual donations to large grants. This means it has little money, but talented people volunteer to help. It is a gift relationship not a contractual one – and as a result the resources available are far higher for Parivartan as a penniless organisation than they would be if it had a middling income.

Our week in Delhi left us reflecting with our Indian hosts on how to scale such activity with the speed necessary to keep up with the massive transitions underway in India. At the same time we discussed the sources of social cohesion in the country – that might hold it together through the storm, but equally might become a source of resistance and conservatism. We also uncovered a deeper question. What if the system cannot deliver what we want it to deliver, because it is founded on a narrow set of assumptions about the human being? This challenge was prompted principally by contact with the artists we visited – who allowed us to see, acknowledge and explore the inner dimensions of life we had experienced in all of our encounters, 'the questions of ultimate concern'.

Varanasi

AT the end of the week a smaller party took the overnight train to Varanasi in Uttar Pradesh, one of the poorest states in India. This is the home state of Rajiv Kumar, who insisted that we come with him to Varanasi – a contrast with Delhi and one of the oldest continually inhabited cities on earth now struggling to cope with the transition to modernity. Our host in the city was another firefly - Navneet Raman, a charismatic young man who returned from a successful career as a stockbroker in Delhi to invest in his city and its people.

At the Vidya Ashram Tenzin Rigzin summed up the condition of India and the world: 'we are all trying to find our roots in this storm'. Driving along the narrow, pot-holed streets of Varanasi another host reminded us of J K Galbraith's view of India as a functioning anarchy. 'It is still an anarchy', he said, 'just no longer functioning'.

At the Jnana Pravaha Centre Mr T K Bhasu told us about the hope to have Varanasi adopted as a world heritage site. 'India is the home of human heritage, and Varanasi is the nerve centre. If any urban centre in the world needs to be saved it is Varanasi, Varanasi, Varanasi'. He repeated the fears about overcrowding in a city of 2m with an infrastructure designed for 200,000: 'If people keep coming to the town, we may need to climb on the shoulders of others to cross the road. This is India's mind, heart and soul. The Ganges sits at the heart of our civilisation. If Ganga dies, civilisation will die. We must de-silt the river and make it deep and wide. The civic authorities have failed.'

We were impressed by the depth these fresh encounters added to our earlier experiences in Delhi. The notion of functioning anarchy was particularly persuasive, suggesting a model of governance in complexity that involves incorporating just enough structure into the messiness to revive functionality, rather than flipping back into dominant, authoritarian control. And we saw the potential value in expanding the networks of hope we had seen in Delhi to embrace the impressive individuals we met in Varanasi, countering the mood of pessimism.

Navneet told us that Varanasi might be ready to learn the lessons of Shiva, the god who destroys in order to recreate. One of the things that Shiva destroys is old habits. We heard some fixed habits of mind that could be shifted: the conviction that nothing can be done, or that nothing works. There is a way of shifting the language towards possibility and aspiration. Parivartan talked about 'meme-bush' rather than ambush.

IFF left India in very reflective mood, conscious of how much we had learned and how little we had to offer. Yet a few months later we were cheered to receive an email from Navneet. 'Thanks to the IFF's catalyst we are now on a path to help the city', he wrote. The City Development Plan had been recalled by the city authorities and taken 'back to the drawing board'. UNESCO had formed a Network of Indian Cities of Living Heritage which Varanasi had joined, and they were planning a special mission to the city. Navneet asked for some IFF materials to distribute to the UNESCO delegates. 'I have been going through the "ten things to do in a conceptual emergency" and the set of cards that IFF gave us. They have been very useful in how I have been able to approach and also negotiate during the last few months'.

IFF remains in contact, nurturing and nurtured by these networks of hope.

Kitbag – growing psychological capacity

IN 2004, with support and encouragement from the World Economic Forum, IFF launched a programme specifically dedicated to addressing the conceptual emergency as it shows up in increasing global levels of mental distress and mental illness.

The programme conducted research into the need for and the nature of psychological capacity – how to trigger the growth response to overwhelm, rather than default neurotic or psychotic responses described in earlier pages and so evident in any news bulletin today. Based on this investigation, the goal of the programme is to develop innovative and cost-effective strategies and tools to enlarge psychological capacity outside care and welfare systems.

One of the first fruits of this programme is Kitbag – the first in a series of interactive products designed to promote self care, resilience and transformational learning. As such, it is not so much a therapeutic as a cultural intervention. Kitbag invites users into an engagement with their inner capacities for real learning, growth and healing. It reminds us that we have inner resources to draw on and that we have a propensity towards wholeness. Kitbag expresses the belief that we live in a world that is ultimately meaningful.

Kitbag was first developed in response to an invitation to present IFF's psychological capacity work at a joint UK/US government symposium in 2005 on handling the psychological aftermath of traumatic events such as 9/11, the Asian tsunami and the London bombings. Some of the delegates flew in directly from New Orleans, having been dealing with the aftermath of Katrina.

Kitbag was welcomed as a prompt for developing inner resources in ways that do not require the intervention of a trained professional. Lessons from disaster relief worldwide have shown that one of the surest routes to recovery is for those affected to help others and in doing so help themselves. This brings out the inner strength in people – a significant resource whose development is often constrained by inappropriate reliance on support services. Kitbag feeds this more person-centred worldview.

Encouraged by this exposure, Kitbag has since been tested and developed in a number of settings where people are under stress, including Cornton Vale Women's Prison, a disability forum, a domestic abuse support group, a public service department etc. The feedback has been tremendous and often moving:

> *'At the time of my breakdown, this would have been Utopia for me. I could not speak to people about this or seek advice. The kit suggests insights without preaching...giving pointers to help turn life around.'*

> *'The kit's like having another friend.'*

> *'I would really recommend this kit to anyone. It has helped me greatly as I suffer from depression and I can honestly say it is better than any medication you take for depression. The relaxation CD really does set you free from being in prison. It takes you to another world if only for half an hour. I don't know how I ever coped without the kit as now I know I never could as well again.'*

The care staff at the prison also asked for Kitbags to support themselves and each other – leading to the development of a package of support for organisations wishing to grow the psychological capacity of their staff. One member of staff said how much her 12 year old had benefited from using the kit she had taken home with her – and so we developed Kitbag for Kids.

In 2007 the National Endowment for Science, Technology and the Arts (NESTA) chose to invest in Kitbag as one of ten mental health innovations with high potential in the UK – support which we hope will enable Kitbag to realise its global potential in the years ahead.

Climate change and energy security

Some years ago the UK government published an international energy strategy designed to address the challenge of maintaining secure global energy supplies at the same time as mitigating the impact of climate change. The lead department responsible for pursuing the strategy internationally, the Foreign and Commonwealth Office, engaged IFF to help them articulate and communicate the complexities of the international strategy to others, within and beyond government.

It soon became apparent that addressing the complexities of climate change and energy security is more than a communications exercise. IFF's work to reveal a clearer view of the wider context exposed critically different approaches to each policy area. To caricature the difference: keep liberalised energy markets *open* to manage the complexities of energy supply and security, whilst *intervening* in the market to shift incentives to tackle climate change. Clearly the search for 'win-win' policies that work in both paradigms is likely to result in a very small menu of options.

IFF therefore expanded its work to embrace three other relevant departments – HM Treasury, Department of Environment, Food and Rural Affairs and the Department for Trade and Industry with additional support and participation from Shell. The challenge now was to provide a larger, more generative framework for thinking about energy policy and climate change together that would get beyond a narrow search for policy solutions in the 'win-win' area.

The first step involved holding up a mirror to the existing policy process. We conducted a series of in-depth interviews with senior officials and others closely involved in the policy system (including a number of industrialists). The data gathered were fascinating – not least for the emotional texture, and for the frankness of the interviewees in their lack of faith in the capacity of the existing policy process to realise their shared vision for 2050. We asked the people we had interviewed whether they recognised this description. They said that it was the most honest and vivid representation of the policy process they had seen, revealing what they all thought but no one individual had the courage to say.

This work has shown that an important part of tackling climate change and energy security will be redesigning the policy process and governance arrangements to enable implementation of transformative innovation. There is no shortage of detailed analysis of the problem or of perfect solutions. What is missing is the hard work of governance innovation required to link the two in effective action.

IFF's information mural depicting the UK Government's 'policy labyrinth' has been taken up elsewhere as emblematic of the inadequacy of our current response to big global challenges. As one senior manager put it at the time: 'This is a messy, difficult problem. Even if we had a group of independent, free-thinking, thoughtful people with no egos it would still raise bloody difficult dilemmas.'

IFF itself continues to work on addressing those dilemmas with a range of partners in the climate change and energy domains, at home and abroad. One promising avenue involves examining the energy economy in its own terms: useful energy output achieved per unit of energy input. That equation will eventually turn negative for all our primary energy sources today – coal, oil, gas, uranium. But for other sources, notably solar, the equation is moving in the opposite direction. If we factor in the rapid learning curves of some of the new technologies the results are both startling and encouraging – both hallmarks of an IFF approach. They also suggest there is a far more generative discussion to be had about climate change and energy security, based not on managing scarcity but on transition to new forms of abundance.

Viable rural communities for the future

IN the summer of 2006 IFF was invited to facilitate a workshop for the Carnegie UK Trust's Commission on Rural Community Development. The Commission, under the chairmanship first of Lord David Steel and latterly Dame Diana Brittan, had been conducting an in-depth inquiry into the state of rural communities in the UK and Ireland in order to inform a new Carnegie programme of support. The Commission had just published its interim report – and was conscious that the accumulating evidence had a familiar ring to it. They asked the IFF to provide a wider appreciation of the emerging future context.

IFF encouraged and contributed to a conversation in the Commission that sought both to extend the context of their inquiry (eg to include the relationship between the rural and the urban) and the time horizon for consideration. The workshop was billed as 'taking evidence from the future' – noticing signs of existing transformative practice in tune with the Commission's emerging vision. This was an exercise in re-perceiving the present that in turn freed up courage and imagination to articulate a more inspiring vision of the future. As a result IFF was invited to remain in support of the Commission, helping to work out the implications of the workshop for policy and practice, and for Carnegie's own rural programme.

The Commission's final report, *A Charter for Rural Communities,* was based on a strategic and systemic view of the characteristics of viable communities both now and into the future. It also showed a mature appreciation of the nature of the challenges and dilemmas involved for policy and practice in introducing the new in the presence of the old. Hence it shied away from the usual wish list of recommendations for government action (usually politically implausible and therefore never realised) in favour of a set of enabling conditions for rural community growth and development – many of which are in communities' own hands.

Carnegie itself, inspired by evidence from the future, has committed to establishing and supporting a community of practice over the next five years encouraging the work of existing 'fiery spirits', fleshing out the practical implications of the systemic model, shifting the landscape of traditional rural community development practice to something more future-oriented, asset-based and taking a broader view of the operating environment. In other words, taking insightful action and sustaining networks of hope.

IFF remains a partner in support of the Carnegie programme – providing an international perspective that goes wider than 'rural development' and ensuring that Carnegie's instincts and practice remain at the leading edge, with an orientation towards transformative rather than merely sustaining innovation.

Governance of the long term: radioactive waste

UK Nirex Ltd was set up by the British government in the 1980s to advise on a long term management strategy for the safe handling of the UK's radioactive waste. This involves a complex set of issues touching on science, technology, public perception, governance – and a time horizon that spans tens of thousands of years whilst the waste remains hazardous. It was also seen fundamentally by Nirex as an ethical issue. This is not about paving the way for a new nuclear programme in the UK. It is about the waste that already exists: we have created it and now we have a moral obligation to manage it safely for the foreseeable future.

When IFF started to work with Nirex in 2004 the senior management were struggling to maintain this long term, ethically driven perspective in a short term, distrustful, political and economic culture quite unsuited to issues of this magnitude and longevity. We worked initially on internal coherence – recognising the multiple disciplines and perspectives that existed even within single organisations. One product was a strategy mural, depicting the Nirex strategy in all its subtlety and complexity and running from the early development of the nuclear industry through the near present to the anticipated (preferred) future at which the waste returns to background radiation levels one million years hence.

This representation helped to provide a broader context for coherent action, such that all of the actors within Nirex - the geologists, the ethicists, the social scientists, the government and media relations specialists, the nuclear engineers – could locate their part in a complex web of relationships unfolding over time. That picture could then be shared with other players – government Ministers and civil servants, the nuclear industry, public meetings, consultative committees. It served both as an antidote against denial and the search for false simplicity, and also as a challenge to all concerned to raise their game to the true level of the task.

The mural was soon supplemented by a series of detailed 'argumentation maps' seeking to capture in detail the best possible arguments – propositions and counter-propositions, evidence and disputes – on all aspects of radioactive waste policy. Thus Nirex's stance became less about advocacy and more about coordination – seeking the best thinking from all those concerned, even if it disrupted settled positions.

At least so far the structures of government have not been able to raise their game to Nirex's level – the organisation was absorbed into the new Nuclear Decommissioning Authority in late 2006. But the lessons learned about the governance of the really long term and the handling of complex scientific/ethical issues in the political system may yet prove invaluable as the UK stands on the brink of a new nuclear power programme.

21st Century competencies and the promise of the arts

DURING 2006 IFF was invited to contribute to a multi-year programme
to catalyse a more sustainable arts and cultural sector in the UK. The
programme, Mission Models Money, was funded by Jerwood Charitable
Foundation, Accenture and others. Part of IFF's contribution was to
stretch the vision and transformative intent. As a result the programme
published not one but two final reports – a traditional set of policy
recommendations, case studies etc and a second, inspirational booklet for
advanced practitioners, *Invitation to an Alternative Future.*

Another perspective IFF brought to bear on the programme was the
appreciation that a more sustainable sector would need more sustainable
people – an acknowledgement of our work on the increasingly evident
signs worldwide of burnout, stress, sickness absence and mental illness as
effects of the conceptual emergency. Such problems are particularly acute
in the arts and cultural sector and the creative economy: those US regions
scoring highest on Richard Florida's Global Creativity Index, for example,
also display the highest incidence of mental distress and psychological
disorder.

If the capacity to thrive in our new environment depends on developing
new competencies, new habits of heart and habits of mind, how might the
leaders of organisations in the arts and cultural sector develop in this way?
Our suggestion was that the 21st century competencies we are interested in
can only be demonstrated and developed by leaders and senior personnel
in situ, in their organisational settings. And that as the capacity of senior
personnel develops in this way so will the organisational setting.

We have tested this thinking over a number of years in a series of
'shadowing' encounters with chief executives in different sectors –
public, private, voluntary and the arts. In each shadowing engagement
a team consisting of a psychotherapist and one other person spend a day
observing both the personal interactions of the CEO and the details and
influence of the setting they work in.

The findings of this work suggest that the arts and cultural sector provides both the most promising organisational settings for the development of 21st century people, and some very impressive existing senior performers. There thus appears to be a remarkable and little recognised opportunity for the arts and cultural sector to take a lead in helping the world to understand how to develop the capacities needed to handle conceptual emergency and the creative settings in which those capacities flourish.

This insight has won the attention and participation of a number of impressive individuals and organisations in the sector, including the National Theatre in London and the Watershed Media Centre in Bristol. Such organisations, ready to make the development of 21st century competencies a core part of their mission, have now become prominent sites for IFF's continuing exploration of creative organisational forms and the future of education.

Near Misses

THE vast majority of IFF's practice, and all of the examples included in these pages, arise from an initial contact with someone who instinctively recognises that it is a conceptual emergency that stands between them and effective action. IFF is invited in to help.

There are cases, however, where such an invitation has not led to a successful IFF project. As might be expected, these cases have been equally instructive in articulating how to put the ten things to do into practice.

We have learned that the sense of conceptual emergency is always personal, and first felt by an individual. But it is often difficult to communicate to the rest of the organisation. Whilst it is always possible to design a shared experience to illuminate the circumstance, it is not so easy to articulate it in a memo, or to get sufficient organisational buy-in for action. In a number of cases the individuals who have first contacted us go under before we can together muster the resources to respond.

One senior manager in a global corporation, conscious of the organisation in over its head and falling into the neurotic response, nevertheless failed to persuade the head of HR to summon help and was shortly thereafter herself on long term sick leave. Another director in a big city council got in touch with IFF saying that the city was unable to cope with the pace of change – or the volume of incoming investment – and was 'swimming in a soup of governance'. That same soup made it impossible, over the course of a year, to schedule any collective exploration of the problem in the face of more pressing events. The director now works for another organisation.

This email provides another vivid example:

> *'I am sorry to say that I have resigned. As I feared the predictable, bureaucratic route is poised to destroy all that is good about this organisation. There is no genuine desire to look to the future or to think*

outside of the boxes and so I decided that life was too short to keep hitting my head against a brick wall. Sadly, I was not alone in that view and two other Board members have resigned. My concerns for the welfare of older people continue to grow and so I think I might now concentrate on writing for publication and also do a bit of political lobbying. Thank you for your support.'

These experiences have taught us a number of lessons, among them the following:

1. being in a conceptual emergency is a personal condition, not an abstract one, and you cannot respond to a conceptual emergency until you acknowledge you are in one;

2. conceptual emergencies are acknowledged by many organisations but often are a product of the fact no single organisation has a budget line or a sense of responsibility for them;

3. it is better to respond by taking action, at any scale, rather than planning to take action – because action triggers learning.

We have learned that for complex social/political problems 'forming the client' ready to engage with the problem is a large part of the work. And we have learned the virtues of starting small and seizing the moment. A natural tendency with big problems is to look for big answers – and it always takes time to pull together the plans, build the relationships and form the coalitions necessary for big action. In today's world we often do not have that time: a crucial contact falls sick, a critical organisation changes its CEO, political attention moves on elsewhere. Fragility and interruption are features of our world. Whilst conceptual emergencies require patient attention, we also need the capacity for rapid response, fast and frugal, to kick start a different learning cycle into motion.

Epilogue

THE ideas in this little book are rooted in IFF's process of social learning over several years. There is little that is entirely new. What is unique is IFF's capacity to bring so many diverse, deeply informed perspectives together, both in theory and in practice, and to deploy the emerging body of learning in service of groups striving to master complexity, uncertainty and rapid change.

These are the conditions of conceptual emergency. Individuals in every corporation seeking to marry their higher aspirations for the world with the need to generate commercial results, in every government department struggling to provide care and compassion within a framework of scarcity and political competition, in every community feeling a sense of powerlessness and loss of agency in the face of globalisation and the forces of 'creative destruction', in every place where the models in the head and the stirrings in the heart are at odds – all of these individuals recognise the description of a 'conceptual emergency' and all liberate tremendous energy and potential when encouraged to articulate that emergency and explore the routes out of it.

Over the course of the next twenty-five years we will be forced to confront the consequences of two hundred and fifty years of material progress. We will not be allowed to ignore them as 'unintended consequences' that can be simply ameliorated for very much longer.

The leaders who emerge in this period, to whom we will turn for inspiration and guidance, will be those who are best able to articulate and to embody with authenticity the lineaments of a new approach sketched in these pages. In doing so they will restructure the corporations, the governments, the communities of which they are a part. They will be working with the grain of our emerging futures, promising not utopia but meaning. They will articulate what we already know, and provide the enabling conditions that allow us to live that truth and develop the potential that has lain dormant under the dominant force of reductionist reasoning. They will appear at all levels in organisations and societies and it will be the task of the visionary manager to recognise them and to remove the constraints that hold them back from releasing the potential in others.

We do not describe a vision of the future, but the reality of the set of values, behaviours, attitudes and principles that will allow us to navigate the challenging years ahead. They provide a compass not a map. When allied to a sense of direction and purpose we will see – have already seen – that the possession of this compass restores effectiveness in action, reclaims the right to dream of a better future, rejuvenates the will to take on intractable problems, reshapes the landscape of organisation, and rekindles confidence and hope in powerful times.

IFF Members

Martin Albrow	Formerly Professor of Sociology, State University of New York, Stony Brook, author 'The Global Age: state and society beyond modernity'
Ruth Anderson	Chief Executive, Barataria Foundation, Scotland
Tony Beesley	Conceptual artist and cartoonist
Max Boisot (died 2011)	Professor at ESADE, University of Ramon Llull in Barcelona and Associate Fellow at the Said Business School, University of Oxford. Author of 'Knowledge Assets: securing competitive advantage in the information economy'
Roberto Carneiro	Former Education Minister, President of Grupo Forum, Portugal, UNESCO International Commission on Education for the Twenty-first Century
Napier Collyns	Co-founder, Global Business Network (GBN), California
Thomas Corver	Corver Management Consultancy, former strategy coordinator at ING bank, The Netherlands
Pamela Deans	IFF recorder and ForthRoad Limited, Scotland
Roanne Dods	Producer, International Futures Forum, former Director, Jerwood Charitable Foundation
Kate Ettinger	Senior Fellow, Center for Health Professions, UCSF; Health Care Ethics Consulant-Mediator & Social Change Educator, San Francisco, USA
Jim Ewing	Independent designer of practical strategies and methods for sustained transformational achievement in uncertain times. Author of 'TransforMAP' and 'Council', conceptware and software for organisational development, Seattle, USA
Brian Goodwin (died 2009)	Schumacher College, Devon and Santa Fe Institute, author 'How the Leopard Changed its Spots: the evolution of complexity'
Bo Gyllenpalm	President SITSERV AB, Sweden and faculty member Fielding Graduate University, USA

Mike Hambly	*Director, Head of High Growth Startup, Scottish Enterprise, former Chief Executive, Digital Animations Group, Glasgow*
Margaret Hannah	*Deputy Director of Public Health, NHS Fife, Scotland*
Pat Heneghan	*Director, ForthRoad Limited, Scotland*
David Hodgson	*Co-founder, The Idea Hive and Connective, San Francisco, USA*
Rebecca Hodgson	*Researcher, International Futures Forum*
Tony Hodgson	*Director, Decision Integrity Ltd, World Modelling Research International Futures Forum*
Robert Horn	*Visiting Scholar in the Human Sciences and Technology Advanced Research Institute (H-STAR) at Stanford University and CEO of MacroVU Inc.*
Kees van der Heijden	*Professor at Templeton College, Oxford, author 'Scenarios: the art of strategic conversation'*
Adam Kahane	*Generon Consulting and Reos Partners, author of 'Solving Tough Problems' and 'Power and Love'*
Pat Kane	*Writer, theorist and musician, Glasgow, author 'The Play Ethic'*
Eamonn Kelly	*President, Global Business Network. Author 'Powerful Times: rising to the challenge of our uncertain world'*
Rajiv Kumar	*Director General, Federation of Indian Chambers of Commerce and Industry (FICCI), New Delhi*
Graham Leicester	*Director, International Futures Forum*
David Lorimer	*Programme Director, Scientific and Medical Network, Scotland*
Charles Lowe	*Consultant, Former head of e-government BT*
Wendy Luhabe	*Bridging the Gap, South Africa, author 'Defining Moments: experiences of black executives in South Africa's workplace'*
Andrew Lyon	*Converger, International Futures Forum*
James McCormick	*Scotland Adviser, Joseph Rowntree Foundation*
Arun Maira	*Member, Planning Commission, Government of India*

Wolfgang Michalski	*WM International, formerly Director, OECD International Futures Programme, author 'Capitalising on Change in a Globalising World'*
Maureen O'Hara	*Chair of Psychology Department, National University La Jolla, CA and President Emerita, Saybrook Graduate School, San Francisco*
Aftab Omer	*President, Meridian University, California*
Ian Page	*Former Research Manager / Futurist, HP Corporate Labs.*
David Peat	*Theoretical physicist and Director of the Pari Center for the New Learning, Tuscany, Italy*
Maria Pereira	*Clinton Climate Initiative and former investment manager*
Noah Raford	*Department of Urban Studies and Planning, MIT and Montior/GBN, London*
Nick Rengger	*Professor of Political Theory and International Relations, University of St Andrews, author 'International Relations, Political Theory and the Problem of Order'*
Vineeta Shanker	*Independent Researcher on faiths in the global economy, previously project director World Faiths Development Dialogue*
Bill Sharpe	*Independent researcher in science, technology and society; Visiting Professor, University of the West of England, author 'Economies of Life'*
Daniel Wahl	*Transition Catalyst & Resilience Research, International Futures Forum (Spain, Germany, UK), former Director of Findhorn College*
Jennifer Williams	*Artist and former Director, Centre for Creative Communities, UK*
Mark Woodhouse	*Professor of Philosophy Emeritus at Georgia State University, USA, author 'Paradigm Wars: worldviews for a new age'*
Chris Yapp	*Specialist in technology, policy and innovation and Senior Associate Fellow at the Institute of Governance and Public Management, Warwick Business School.*

Publishers

TRIARCHY Press publishes in the field of organisational and social praxis: the process by which a theory or skill is applied, practised or embodied. We look for the best new thinking on the organisations and social structures we work and live in.

The name 'Triarchy' comes from Gerard Fairtlough's Triarchy Theory, which challenges the hegemony of hierarchy in organisations and puts forward two alternative ways of organising power and responsibility in order to get things done: heterarchy and responsible autonomy.

We publish books, pamphlets, articles, a game and an Idioticon (a glossary) about innovative approaches to designing and steering organisations, the public sector, teams, society ... and the creative lives of individuals. Our publications offer a number of different but related approaches to organisational issues from the fields of systems thinking, design thinking, innovation, cultural theory, complexity, somatics and leadership studies.

Triarchy Press works in partnership with IFF to publish pamphlets and books that share IFF's learning with the global community. To date these are:

In Search of the Missing Elephant by Don Michael
Economies of Life by Bill Sharpe
Ten Things to Do in a Conceptual Emergency by Graham Leicester and Maureen O'Hara
Beyond Survival by Graham Leicester
Transformative Innovation in Education by Graham Leicester, Keir Bloomer and Denis Stewart
Ready for Anything: Designing Resilience for a Transforming World by Tony Hodgson

www.triarchypress.com

International Futures Forum

INTERNATIONAL Futures Forum (IFF) is a non-profit organisation established to support a transformative response to complex and confounding challenges and to restore the capacity for effective action in today's powerful times.

At the heart of IFF is a deeply informed inter-disciplinary and international network of individuals from a range of backgrounds covering a wide range of diverse perspectives, countries and disciplines. The group meets as a learning community as often as possible, including in plenary session. And it seeks to apply its learning in practice.

IFF takes on complex, messy, seemingly intractable issues – notably in the arenas of health, learning, governance and enterprise – where paradox, ambiguity and complexity characterise the landscape, where rapid change means yesterday's solution no longer works, where long-term needs require a long-term logic and where only genuine innovation has any chance of success.

Authors

GRAHAM Leicester is Director of International Futures Forum. He is a former member of HM Diplomatic Service and has subsequently developed a special interest and wide experience in the areas of governance, innovation, education and the arts.

MAUREEN O'Hara, PhD is Professor of Psychology, National University, La Jolla, California, and President Emerita of Saybrook Graduate School and Research Institute, San Francisco. She is Co-Editor of *The Handbook of Person-Centred Psychotherapy and Counselling* and a founder member of IFF.